PUPPIES

Written By: Janie Reinart

Illustrated By: Chris Bigelow

LEVEL — READING **2** GRADES 1 TO 3 LEVEL — READER

bendon®

My eyes shine in the dark.
I talk with a glad bark.
My nose is cold and wet.
I'm your best friend—a pet.

Who am I?
Hint: Turn page to find out...

Answer: I am a puppy.

Puppies are mammals just like us. They have hair, are warm blooded, and drink their mother's milk. They are born in a litter with 2-10 brothers and sisters. Puppies love to snuggle together to keep warm.

Puppy Profile

- Moisture on the nose helps grab hold of scents.
- Their nose sniffs out mom's milk right away.
- Puppies can't see or hear until they are two to three weeks old.
- At three weeks, their first teeth come in and they begin eating solid food.

Pups are ready to leave their mom around 7-12 weeks of age. The average puppy is considered a baby until 4 months of age, a teenager between 6 and 14 months, and an adult by 2 years.

Breed: Springer Spaniel

Breed: Irish Setter

Breed: Mixed

Exercise, good food, loving care, and regular check-ups keep a puppy healthy.

Breed: German Shepherd

Puppy Profile

* Panting helps your pup stay cool.

* A veterinarian (an animal doctor) helps take care of puppies.

* Puppies have an average of 320 bones. Puppies with very long tails have more bones. People have 206 bones.

There are over 150 different breeds of puppies.

Breed: Mountain Cur
Working Group

Breed: Beagle
Hound Group

Breed: Pug
Toy Group

Breed: Manchester Terrier
Terrier Group

Breed: Border Collie
Herding Group

Breed: Labrador Retriever
Sporting Group

Breed: Dalmatian
Non-Sporting Group

Puppies can be very big, very small, or somewhere in between.

The Mastiff is one of the largest dog breeds, with a life span of 6-10 years. Mastiffs are considered puppies for three years.

The Chihuahua is the smallest breed of dog and the longest-lived. Its life span is 12-17 years and it is considered a puppy for two years.

Puppy Profile

🐾 **Mastiff birth weight:**
2 pounds
Adult weight:
up to 190 pounds

🐾 **Chihuahua birth weight:**
2 1⁄2 ounces
Adult weight:
2 pounds

A puppy's fur can be long or short, silky or rough, curly or straight. Their fur can be one solid color, or a mixture of colors including white, brown, black, red, gray, or yellow.

Breed: Norfolk Terrier

Breed: Border Collie

Puppy Profile

- Puppies from the same litter are often different colors!
- The bigger a puppy's paw, the larger he will grow.

Breed: Afghan Hound

Breed: Bulldog

Breed: West Highland White Terrier

Puppies learn by playing, just like babies do. Puppies are teething until 6 months of age. Chew toys and rawhide bones can keep a puppy busy for hours, and may prevent them from ruining shoes, toys, clothes, and furniture.

Breed: Labrador Retriever

Puppy Profile

- ❖ Puppies love to dig!
- ❖ They dig to bury or retrieve bones.
- ❖ They dig to make a "cooling" pit to lie in when it's hot outside.

Breed: Mixed

Puppies use their voice, eyes, face, and body to communicate.

Breed: Mixed

A mother dog whimpers into her puppy's fur. This is dog talk for "listen to me and mind your manners".

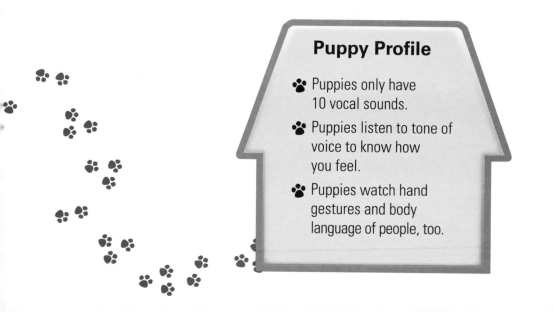

Puppy Profile

- Puppies only have 10 vocal sounds.
- Puppies listen to tone of voice to know how you feel.
- Puppies watch hand gestures and body language of people, too.

Breed: Beagle

Can you tell what these puppies are thinking?

A glad bark and a wagging
tail mean, "I'm happy."

Breed: Mixed

Perky ears say,
"I hear something.
What's going on?"

Breed: Samoyed

If I am lying on my back it means, "You're the boss."

Breed: Dachshund

A whine and anxious eyes say, "I need something."

A deep growl and a piercing stare mean, "Look out, I'm angry."

Breed: Rhodesian Ridgeback

Breed: Chihuahua

Some puppies are trained to be service dogs for people with disabilities. Seeing eye dogs or guide dogs help blind people get around in the world, and hearing dogs alert deaf people to fire alarms, doorbells, and even crying babies.

Breed: Labrador Retriever

Puppy Profile

- Labrador Retrievers, Golden Retrievers, and German Shepherds are the most common service dogs.

- Puppies are placed in foster families at 8 weeks of age.

- Puppies begin formal training around 18 months of age.

- Formal training takes 4-6 months.

Amazing Puppy Facts

The Chow is the only dog that has a black tongue. Pink at birth, it changes to a blue-black color by the time the puppy is 8 weeks old.

Siberian Huskies can have brown, hazel, or a sky blue eye color. It is not uncommon for this puppy to have two different colored eyes.

The Basenji doesn't bark, but talks in a howl that sounds like a yodel.

The Newfoundland is an expert swimmer and has webs between its toes.

Be loving and caring, gentle and kind. I will always be your faithful friend, will you be mine?